# Mary Robinson

## Citizen of the World

By Gerald Colman Jones

John Gordon Burke Publisher, Inc.

# Contemporary Profiles and Policy Series for the Younger Reader

## Library of Congress Cataloging-in-Publication Data

Jones, Gerald Colman, 1930–

Mary Robinson : citizen of the world / by Gerald Colman Jones.

p. cm. — (Contemporary profiles and policy series for the younger reader)

Includes bibliographical references and index.

ISBN 0–934272–64–6 (paper : alk. paper). — ISBN 0–934272–63–8 (cloth : alk. paper)

1. Robinson, Mary, 1944– 2. Women presidents—Ireland—Biography—Juvenile literature. 3. Presidents—Ireland—Biography—Juvenile literature. 4. Women diplomats—Ireland—Biography—Juvenile literature. 5. Diplomats—Ireland—Biography—Juvenile literature. 6. Women civil rights workers—Biography—Juvenile literature. 7. Civil rights workers—Biography—Juvenile literature. [1. Robinson, Mary, 1944– 2. Presidents—Ireland. 3. Diplomats. 4. Civil rights workers. 5. Women—Biography.] I. Title. II. Series.

DA965.R63 J66 2000

941.50824'092–dc21

[B]                                                                 00–062100

Credits: Cover Design: Tissi Blount/M&H Design; Photographs: Arus an Uachtarain; United Nations Office of the High Commissioner for Human Rights.

# TABLE OF CONTENTS

Chapter 1: The Beginning . . . . . . . . . . . . . . . . . . . . . . . . . . . . . 5

Chapter 2: Early Family Life . . . . . . . . . . . . . . . . . . . . . . . . 11

Chapter 3: On to America . . . . . . . . . . . . . . . . . . . . . . . . . . 16

Chapter 4: Finding Her Career . . . . . . . . . . . . . . . . . . . . . 21

Chapter 5: Beginning Family Life . . . . . . . . . . . . . . . . . . . 25

Chapter 6: Politics Beckoned . . . . . . . . . . . . . . . . . . . . . . . 28

Chapter 7: The Lawyer Emerges . . . . . . . . . . . . . . . . . . . . 34

Chapter 8: High Honors Achieved . . . . . . . . . . . . . . . . . . . 39

Chapter 9: Mary's Challenge—Transforming The
    Presidency . . . . . . . . . . . . . . . . . . . . . . . . . . . . . . . . . . . 43

Chapter 10: From Ireland to the World . . . . . . . . . . . . . . . 49

Chapter 11: Career Highlights . . . . . . . . . . . . . . . . . . . . . . 52

Appendix: A Brief History of Ireland . . . . . . . . . . . . . . . . . 57

Chronology . . . . . . . . . . . . . . . . . . . . . . . . . . . . . . . . . . . . . 62

Glossary of Terms . . . . . . . . . . . . . . . . . . . . . . . . . . . . . . . 65

To Learn More . . . . . . . . . . . . . . . . . . . . . . . . . . . . . . . . . . 68

Index . . . . . . . . . . . . . . . . . . . . . . . . . . . . . . . . . . . . . . . . . . 70

*Mary Robinson*

*—President of Ireland, 1990-1997*

# THE BEGINNING: CHAPTER ONE

A look at Ireland's history

Politics has always been a man's game. At least until the twentieth century. Then, a few women in a handful of countries reached positions of political power. Women such as Queen Elizabeth I in England and Queen Cleopatra of Egypt inherited thrones. But that is not the same thing as gaining power by working at it through the political system. Only an unusual woman can even try to break in, and only a very unusual woman can succeed–even though women make up at least one half the population.

Indira Gandhi in India and Margaret Thatcher in the United Kingdom were rare exceptions to the male dominance of politics. And in Ireland, there had never been a woman who had aimed at, and achieved, a major political office such as the Presidency. That is, until Mary Robinson came along.

What was so special about Mary Robinson? Well, for one thing, it never occurred to her to feel that any professional ambition open to a man should be out of bounds for a woman. Then, she was also both intelligent and hard–working.

Mary Robinson's sincerity was so obvious that she had little difficulty in convincing people to accept her point of view when she was right. And most of the time she usually was right. She also looked around to find things that were not right, and then set about to change those things.

But how did Mary Robinson reach this point? It is really quite a remarkable story. Given the time and place into which she was born, no one could have predicted the extraordinary and unexpected course of her life. No one could have predicted the particular battles she would fight and win, and no one could have known how much she would influence her own country and the world. Nobody at all.

Mary Robinson was born in the little town of Ballina. Ballina is a small town situated on a little river in the most western province in Ireland. In the 1940s, there cannot have been a great deal happening there; the town itself is known for being dull and remote. And at the time, the whole country of Ireland was in a state of quietness bordering on boredom.

Although the World War II was raging in Europe and across the Pacific, and London was being bombed by the German Luftwaffe (Air Force) and by unmanned missiles aimed from Holland and Belgium, it was not to be found in Ireland.

The Irish Prime Minister, Eamon de Valera (born in New York to a Spanish father and Irish mother), who had spent time in British prisons during the Irish struggle for independence from Britain, was not inclined to help Great Britain during her struggle for survival. He kept the country officially neutral.

Ireland, however, indirectly helped the Allied cause through exports of food to England. Two hundred thousand young Irish men joined the British Armed Forces to fight for England, and thousands more went to work in British munitions factories, replacing British workers who had already joined the armed forces.

But inside Ireland itself, it seemed as if nothing out of the ordinary was happening. Food was plentiful; the country was reasonably prosperous; and except for shortages of a few commodities like tea and whatever had usually been imported from Europe, people living in the Irish Free

State (later to become the Republic of Ireland) felt little impact from the war.

In fact, among the members of both houses of the Irish parliament, there was only one person who constantly repeated, both inside and outside parliament, that Ireland should lay aside, for the time being, its old antagonism to England, and join the Allies in the war against Nazi Germany.

Although Ireland was not a military power, its neutrality meant the British navy was not able to use important ports in the west of Ireland, such as Galway and Cobh (Queenstown), as bases to defend the ship convoys, carrying munitions and other supplies from the U.S.A. and Canada, against the German submarines.

Many in Ireland wondered why the British, who had troops in Northern Ireland, did not simply invade southern Ireland to take over and use these ports. But the British did not want to be seen to be willing to invade neutral countries like the Germans had done to Belgium, Holland and Denmark. Besides, hoping that the United States would enter the war on its side, Great Britain did not want to anger Irish–Americans and give them good reason to use their influence to dissuade the United States from becoming involved in the war.

Politics in Ireland was dominated by the Fianna Fail party, under the strong control of Eamon de Valera. The bitter memories of the civil war, which had ended nearly twenty years earlier, were still to be found in the political life of the time.

The civil war in Ireland had started in 1922, almost immediately after the establishment of the Irish Free State. The elected government of the Free State accepted the treaty which ended the "war of independence" which was basically a guerilla war, but at the price of the six counties of Ulster (Northern Ireland) remaining part of the United Kingdom of Great Britain and Northern Ireland, which it still is.

In addition, the British monarch continued to be the head of state, although represented in Ireland by the British Governor–General, as is the case in Canada and other British Dominions at the present time.

The question of the treaty was put to a referendum, and accepted by the majority of the voters, who wanted peace and were tired of fighting. However there was a substantial minority, led by Eamon de Valera, who refused to accept the treaty, and a civil war followed, which dragged on for about three years, and was neither won nor lost by either side.

Religion, which meant the Roman Catholic Church, was still a major influence on both political and social issues. The Roman Catholic hierarchy of bishops and arch–bishops had enough influence to have a prohibition of divorce enshrined in the 1937 Constitution. The importation of contraceptives was a criminal offense, as was homosexual practice and abortion.

The practice of religion other than Catholicism was not at all interfered with or discouraged. Protestants and Jews were not discriminated against, although neither community played any significant role in politics. This was because of the small size of both communities, but also out of prudence.

Protestants had come to be identified with the historic enemy, England, even though Irish Protestants had played a notable role in the fight for Irish independence over the centuries. Jews lived quietly and unobtrusively, although there had never been in Ireland any overt anti–semitism.

Trinity College, Dublin, founded as a Protestant university by Queen Elizabeth 1, continued to flourish, although very few Catholics attended, being forbidden by most bishops to do so.

The Irish language, a form of Gaelic, survived as the spoken language in a few remote areas, but was a major preoccupation of the government and educational authorities. In an effort to preserve and extend its use, the government insisted that it be the medium of instruction in primary schools, even though most students, and most teachers, spoke it badly. Even the politicians, with the exception of Eamon de Valera and a few others, were not fluent in it, although most of them did not readily admit it.

The Irish language was extremely difficult to learn, and, because of historical circumstances, contained practically no scientific, medical or business vocabulary. Nevertheless, the first Irish President, Douglas Hyde, was appointed to his position because he was the foremost living scholar of Irish, both modern and medieval.

This occurred, in spite of the fact that he was a Protestant and the son of a Protestant minister. Furthermore, he had no particular interest or involvement in politics, had not been a part of the struggle for Irish independence, nor a supporter of either side in the civil war which followed independence for the south of Ireland. All of this, however was to his advantage. As he was not indebted to any political party, he therefore could be supported by all.

The Presidency, as designed by the 1937 Constitution, was to have no power, and practically no influence. It was a purely figure–head office, replacing that of the

Governor–General, who had previously represented the British monarch in Ireland, and after the establishment of the Irish Free State, had no power or influence either.

The President could not even leave the State without the permission of the government, and never did. He lived in the same house that was previously occupied by the Governor–General. The President received ambassadors, signed laws, entertained people, but never said or did anything to disturb politics. He was as powerless as the President of Switzerland, whose name a great many Swiss don't even know.

While officially the head of the Irish state, the President got little popular or media attention which was, and indeed still is lavished on the British Royal family, whose every move was reported at length in the Irish press. Indeed a sarcastic Irishman said it wouldn't matter if the President even spread marmalade on his breakfast sausages; no one would pay any attention.

However on May 21st 1944 in Ballina, a baby girl was born who would change all that.

## EARLY FAMILY LIFE: CHAPTER TWO

Mary and her Family

Mary Robinson could not be described in any way as a disadvantaged child. Her parents were affluent and well–connected. They were also kind to others, especially to their children, and of their children most of all to Mary, the only girl of five children.

Something has been made of the fact Mary was the middle child, with two older and two younger brothers, as if this somehow explained her intelligence, ambition and idealism. But her brothers were also bright, industrious and intended for professional careers like their parents. Her two elder brothers became doctors; her two younger brothers became, like Mary herself, lawyers. This was typical of Irish middle–class families at the time, for a young person would not have gone into business unless there had been a family business to take over.

Mary's ancestry was not uncommon either. It was a mixture of Gaelic, English and Norman–French which make up the majority of the Irish people. No doubt, there were also traces of Scottish, Scandinavian and of the pre–Celtic inhabitants who survived as a distinct people with their own language at least until the 11th century A.D.

Owing to the turbulence which followed the Norman invasions of Ireland in the twelfth century, genealogical records were rare. Mary's father, however, was descended from a Norman–French family (the Bourkes) that had settled in County Mayo since the thirteenth century. Her mother's family lived in County Donegal, and the family name was O'Donnell. This was the same name as that of the Earl Hugh O'Donnell of Donegal, who fled to Spain after the final defeat of the Stuarts (briefly kings of England) at the Battle of the Boyne in 1690.

Mary attended a local private day–school in her home town of Ballina until she was ten years old. Her mother felt it was more suitable for Mary than the public school that most children attended.

Mary, however, needed to get away from Ballina. "I couldn't wait to escape to boarding–school." She also was to say: "I couldn't wait to escape to college. I couldn't wait to escape."

Her first escape, at the age of ten, was to Mount Anville, a leading girls' school run by Sacred Heart nuns at Dundrum, County Dublin. Mary did well there and felt there that she wanted to be a nun. There was a high–minded austerity about the nuns which appealed to her.

She admired how important for the nuns it was to be committed to working for social justice. This was something that impressed her at the time and which she was to remember later.

But Mount Anville was a school for the elite, where boarders were not allowed to speak to the day pupils. She did not understand why she did not question it more: "I questioned it, but I never really took it on. We didn't mix with the day pupils, and that was pure snobbery."

Mary did not send her own daughter to Mount Anville, partly for those reasons.

At Mount Anville, Mary gained attention there by being "irritatingly good" at everything. Her personality, even at that young age, was warm and attractive. It was entirely normal for young girls and boys of upper class families to be sent to private schools, since there was no education beyond age fourteen available in the public schools.

What contact Mary had with children of working–class

families was gained back home in Ballina before she went to boarding school, and during her school holidays. But even at a young age she was struck by the disparities between the life of the middle class and of working people, and it seemed to her, even then, to be unjust.

At the end of her years at Mount Anville, her parents sent her to Paris to a snobbish finishing school, Mlle Anita Pojninska's in the 16th Arrondissement. This was a bit unusual, though not exceptional for young middle class Irish girls. This experience left Mary with an abiding love of France, and exceptional fluency in the French language.

In Paris, she enjoyed a new sense of intellectual freedom where she was able to read books banned in Ireland. She became a compulsive reader and felt very much at home in Paris. It was here that Mary decided to become a lawyer, believing it might be the expeditious road to justice in society. During her stay in Paris, her grandfather H.C. Bourke died, but she didn't have the money to go to his funeral.

On her return from Paris, she spent a year at home in Ballina studying for the Trinity College entrance exam. She gained a scholarship, and then entered Trinity College, Dublin.

Since it was considered a Protestant university, and had been founded as such, her parents sought permission from the archbishop of Dublin for her to attend. Of course she could have gone there anyway, as some Catholics did, but no doubt her parents felt it was better to take these steps.

Mary's two elder brothers had attended Trinity College with the permission of the local bishop, but Archbishop McQuaid of Dublin had extended his ban on enrollment at Trinity College over the whole country. It was for this reason that his permission was sought and obtained by her parents.

While a university student, Mary lived in a house in Westland Row, Dublin purchased by her parents for her brothers and Anne Coyne, who had been her Mary's nanny. Mary was a serious student and did not participate in her brothers' student social life. She had left–wing political views; they didn't. Mary had her 21st birthday party at Westland Row, and it was a formal dinner party. At the time, her closest female friend was the poet Eavan Boland, whose father was a senior Irish diplomat who presided over the United Nations General Assembly.

Within the faculty of law at Trinity College, Mary immediately distinguished herself by her skill in the debating society, and her proficiency in her studies. She co–edited the Irish Student Law Review and also served as Secretary of the Students Union.

At Trinity College, Mary met Nicholas Robinson, a cultivated, and "respectable Protestant young man", in the same law class. He also took first–class honors in his first year. Nicholas was artistic and adept at drawing cartoons of political figures which were published in one of Ireland's national newspapers. They became good friends, and a few years later were married.

In her second year at Trinity College, Mary won another scholarship; she disliked certain restrictions on women at Trinity College, so started visiting University College Dublin, the Catholic university. Her inaugural address as auditor of Trinity's Law Society in February 1967 was entitled "Law and Morality". Her theme in this address was "the separation of church and state, [and] the argument that the constitution and laws of the Irish state should not reflect the moral teaching of one church". On these grounds she attacked Ireland's laws on divorce, contraception, suicide, and capital punishment. Human rights in Ireland, she believed, were too restricted.

Mary was awarded an honors degree in law, and attracted sufficient attention to receive a Fellowship at Harvard University in the United States. It would not be the last time that she would be recognized by this distinguished educational institution in the United States.

## ON TO AMERICA: CHAPTER THREE
The American Experience

It is impossible to exaggerate the importance of the United States of America to Ireland. The reasons for this importance lies in the history of Ireland and in the minds of the Irish people.

As early as the American War of Independence and the founding of the United States in 1776, the Irish looked across the Atlantic. They saw what a determined nation could do to rid itself of control by an Imperial power.

The Americans had not wanted to be a colony. They were not content to be just a resource, a source of revenue through taxation and a source of material for England's manufacturing industries.

Neither were the Irish. Although Ireland was, on paper, part of the United Kingdom of Great Britain and Ireland, in reality it was little more than a colony, where Irish interests were secondary to those of England. They saw that among the signatories of the American Declaration of Independence there were Irishmen, that Irishmen had fought in large numbers for that independence, and took their place in the building of the Republic. Could they not do the same for their own country?

The disastrous famines in the 1840s in Ireland emphasized the importance of the American connection. Famine relief from America materially helped alleviate suffering in Ireland, at a time when the British government had decided to do nothing. The willingness of the United States to accept massive numbers of Irish emigrants, eventually amounting to millions, saved their lives.

The poverty and illiteracy of the majority of these immigrants resulted in a certain degree of discrimination against them initially. However, by their own hard work and energy as well as by their interest in politics and their awareness of its importance, they rose up gradually, as did all the other waves of America's immigrants, to become a community of significance in the American mosaic.

The election of John F. Kennedy as President established the fact that they had arrived. Eamon de Valera, who was a leader in Ireland's own war of independence and later a leader of their government, had been born in New York, with an Irish mother and a Spanish father. The Irish had never doubted that the United States had been and continued to be essential to the well–being of Ireland.

When Mary Robinson went to the United States for the first time in 1967, she was twenty–three years old. She would have been aware of these historical links with the United States, even though her own family history had been more connected with England. She had emerged from Trinity College top of her class and a qualified barrister or lawyer. At the same time she had obtained a Fellowship for a year at Harvard University.

Her year at Harvard University was an eye–opener for her. She loved the sense of freedom to think what she liked and say what she thought. In Ireland, people were more careful. She was pleased that even students cared about the improvement of American society as a whole.

At the time, the civil rights movement was in full swing. She saw how the Constitution of the United States was being used to address wrongs in society. She learnt that politics and the law could be used to improve the condition of poor people and of people who suffered discrimination. She was to learn these lessons well.

In the classes she attended at Harvard there were

lawyers and law students from all over the United States and every continent: Asia, Europe, Africa, Australia, North and South America. These international contacts made her aware of legal and human rights problems all over the world. While at Harvard she obtained a Master's degree in law.

In order to get her degree, she had to write a paper on a legal subject. She wrote about what she knew, the legal system of Europe, which was just beginning to unite into the community of nations, in something like the way the various American states united to become the United States of America.

She could see that what she had learnt at Harvard about the power of law and of the constitution properly applied, could be used back home in Ireland. One of the advantages of studying or working abroad is to see and learn about things that are different than they are at home, and she intended to use what she had learnt at Harvard to make Ireland a better place.

At the same time, she took herself less seriously than many of the other students. She was young, and felt she should have some fun. She had some fun in the usual ways, but as well, she enjoyed taking part in more serious activities. This was the time of student demonstrations against the Vietnamese War, and demonstrations in support of the civil rights movement.

She joined in sit–ins at Harvard Law School where she took all kinds of courses: Urban Legal Studies, the American Constitution, Federal and State law. She also visited Boston and New York. She saw in these cities evidence of poverty, racism and drug addiction.

This was the time in which President Lyndon Johnson

started poverty and civil rights programs. She was at Harvard when Martin Luther King and Robert F. Kennedy were assassinated in April and June 1968. This violence horrified her and was new to her, as the violence in the North of Ireland had not begun.

Mary carried the lessons she had learned at Harvard back to Ireland including the importance of a federal system for the creation of the European Union. This allowed a European Court of Justice to be superior to the Irish Supreme Court, so that it could reverse decisions of the latter.

Of more significance to her personally, however, was the self–confidence of the Harvard students. She admired their inclination to take political action in spite of their young age, and in this she was to follow their example.

Nearly twenty years later, the value of her time in the United States was reinforced when, as President of Ireland, she entertained in December 1995 the President Bill Clinton and his wife Hillary at Arus an Uachtarain, her official residence.

President Clinton suggested that she pay a state visit to the United States some time soon. She was delighted, but of course as President of Ireland she would have to have the permission of the government to go.

She felt in many ways very close to the Clintons, because of the similarity of their backgrounds in law and in being educated at New England universities. But the head of the Irish government at the time, John Bruton, didn't want her to go.

Perhaps understandably, politicians didn't want Mary to share in the limelight, since President Clinton had been involved in the Northern Ireland peace process, as they had. However Bill Clinton announced publicly in Dublin that he was looking forward to her state visit. As a result, Mary went to Washington, D.C. as a visiting head of state in June of 1996.

## FINDING HER CAREER: CHAPTER FOUR
### The Beginnings of Professional Life

On her return from Harvard, Mary joined the teaching staff of the Trinity College school of law. She was appointed Reid Professor of Criminal and Constitutional Law. This was a part–time job with a five–year term, designed mainly to help the most bright and promising young law graduates to earn some money while they started their legal careers.

Without this, she would have had to depend on her parents for financial support. She gave more time and energy to this work than she had to, but then, this was the way Mary was.

While a student in her first year at Trinity, she had met a creative, intelligent law student, Nicholas Robinson. He was good at drawing caricatures and cartoons of political figures, which were published in one of the national newspapers, the Irish Times. He was her future husband, Nicholas, whom she married in December 1970, and with whom she subsequently had her three children.

In 1969, with Nick's encouragement, she decided to run for election by Trinity College as one of its three representatives to the Senate. The Irish Senate in no way resembled the American Senate, being little more than a debating society.

It could propose laws, provided no public money was required to put them into effect, but without the consent of the Dail, (pronounced Doyle), which was the other and more important house of parliament, such proposals could get no further. Furthermore, of the sixty Senate members, eleven were appointed by the government, only six by the two universities, and the rest by various local authorities, who tended to vote along political party lines.

The chances of an independent (i.e. someone not belonging to a major political party) getting elected were not that good. But the Senate was valuable as a place where unpopular opinions could be heard. Because it could propose laws, it could get controversial subjects debated. It could even sometimes force the government to introduce legislation of its own on the question that had been raised in the Senate.

The voters, between six and seven thousand in number, were all the graduates of Trinity College, who were scattered all over Ireland, including Northern Ireland, Great Britain and the entire English–speaking world. The election was by mail. Her friends, including her school–friends from Mount Anville and her colleagues at Trinity, conducted an intense letter–writing campaign on her behalf. On account of the greater mobility of the younger graduates, it is likely that the voters were primarily older, well–established men and women.

Trinity College had never elected a woman or a Catholic to the Senate before. She had the reputation of being a feminist and a political radical. However at the time of her first election campaign neither of these labels did her much harm, given the spirit of the times. In the sixties, even conservative Ireland was not entirely immune to the revolutionary winds blowing over the world.

Mary ran for election as an independent, rather than aligning herself with either of the two big political parties which had formed governments up to that point. She appealed to women, to the young, to the politically liberal but also to the more intelligent of the older generation. She rounded up an impressive list of supporters, including professors and bishops, predominantly Protestant. She hoped to get the votes of women.

To do this, she had to concentrate on issues which affected women mainly, marriage, divorce and contraception. She believed that women should be free to choose. If they couldn't, they weren't free. Of course, in Ireland at that time, women weren't really free. If they choose to get married, they had to leave their jobs if they worked for any public body. They had no right to equal pay, and earned barely half of what men did. A married woman's husband was the legal guardian of their children. He got the childrens' allowances from the state. If his wife worked and paid income tax, he got any rebates she was owed. Women were definitely discriminated against.

By being vocal about these issues, she undoubtedly attracted many women's votes. On August 12th 1969 she was elected as the third of the Trinity College Senators.

Her election to the Senate in 1969 came at a time when Northern Ireland was in a state of turmoil. The Catholic minority in Northern Ireland were beginning to express their resentment at being discriminated against. They had difficulty in getting jobs, in getting housing and education.

The more they demonstrated and agitated, the more likely they were to be put in prison. The police at that time were almost all Protestant. It is hard for us now to imagine how a difference in religion could affect almost every aspect of life. But it did, and the differences in the end led to violence and murder.

People all over Ireland feared the future, and they had good reason for their fear. Once the killing started, it was hard to stop. It has continued until very recent years, and could break out again. Mary Robinson was, from the beginning, very concerned about and very involved with the situation in Northern Ireland.

## BEGINNING FAMILY LIFE: CHAPTER FIVE

Marriage and Children

Nicholas Robinson had met Mary Bourke when they were both first–year students at Trinity College in the law faculty. His family had moved to Ireland from England in the 18th century. Two of his uncles were killed in the Second World War, fighting in the British Air Force. He had other relatives who had worked for the British government and for the British Royal family.

Nicholas' father Howard was a successful banker in Dublin with his own bank, and lacked for nothing. As well as his house near Dublin, he had a holiday home in Tenerife. He was involved in the community and was on the finance committee of the Church of Ireland. He was also a director of one of the national newspapers, the Irish Times.

Nick had three brothers. His mother had died when he was ten years old, and he and his brothers were brought up by their father who at one point took the entire family on a tour of Canada and the United States. Howard was generous to his children, and as a young man at Trinity, Nicholas had the advantage of a substantial allowance, so that in comparison to other students he was quite rich.

From the time of their first meeting, Nick showed an interest in Mary Bourke, and appealed to her fun–loving side. He was not as seriously interested in his studies as she was, although he did very well at them. He was more interested in history, art, and in having a good time.

In addition to being very creative, Nick was a keen cartoonist, and his political cartoons were regularly published in one of the national newspapers. This, however, did not endear him to Mary's parents, who felt he was an unsuitable prospective husband for their daughter.

Mary's parents did what they could to discourage the relationship, insisting on separations during his courtship of her. They would have preferred someone who was well established, and were aware of the cultural, financial and religious differences between them.

In spite of her parents opposition, however, Mary accepted Nicholas' proposal of marriage, and the wedding took place on December 12, 1970. The ceremony was performed at a catholic church in Dublin. In view of the fact that Nick was a Protestant, the permission of the Archbishop of Dublin had to be obtained. No member of her family attended, and Mary and Nick flew to Paris for their honeymoon.

In spite of her parents' reservations, the marriage was to be a wonderful success for both of them. They were totally compatible with each other, complementing the other to an unusual degree.

Nick was not as ambitious as Mary was, and had no difficulty with the fact that she always earned more than he did, although he earned a good income as a solicitor or lawyer. Much of his time and energy was taken up with interests such as the preservation of the architectural heritage of Dublin.

Dublin is an old city, and most of the central part of it was built in the eighteenth century, on both sides of the river Liffey. The north side was originally the more fashionable part, but at the beginning of the 18th century, the duke of Leinster, the leader of Dublin society at the time, decided to move across the river and build a town house. Other members of the aristocracy soon followed. The duke's house, Leinster House, is still there. In this part of Dublin, one now finds the seat of the Irish government.

In addition to historic preservation in this part of Dublin, the Robinson's were also involved in the attempt to preserve Wood Quay. It was the site of a Viking settlement in Dublin from the tenth century. While this attempt was ultimately unsuccessful, in spite of public protests and even sit–ins, the destruction of the site was delayed long enough to allow archaeological excavation and documentation of the ancient settlement.

Another fortunate result for Mary in the struggle to preserve Wood Quay was her introduction to Bride Rosney, who was a prominent activist in the campaign for the preservation of the Irish medieval architectural heritage. She became a loyal friend to Mary and the godmother of their youngest child two years later.

Nicholas and Mary had three children: Tessa, born in 1972, William in 1974, and Aubrey in 1981. In spite of their frantically busy lives, the children were brought up with the same devoted care and attention that Mary and Nicholas had both received from their own parents.

Family life was enormously important to both of them. The family included not just them and their children, but their relatives and even some of their closest friends.

In her political and her legal work, Mary stressed over and over again the welfare of the family ought to be the primary objective of the State and of the legal system. She used every mention of the word "family" in the Irish Constitution and the laws of Ireland to strengthen her arguments for this position.

## POLITICS BECKONED: CHAPTER SIX

Challenges of a Political Career

Mary realized that governments could oppress people, and that some governments all over the world were depriving people of their human rights. She also could see that organized religion, especially the religion of the majority of the people, had the potential also to be oppressive. At the same time, she saw that governments in other countries could and did work towards making people secure, prosperous and free, and that religion is, generally, a positive moral force in society.

In 1976, Mary decided to pursue seriously a career in politics. But as things turned out, she had a very difficult time in achieving much of anything through political means.

Mary had been elected to the Irish legislature in 1969, at the astonishingly young age of twenty–five. She was one of the representatives of Trinity College to the Senate, and she retained that seat through numerous general elections until 1989, when she decided not to run for election again.

She joined the Irish Labour Party in 1976. She had felt that the Labour Party was probably more sympathetic to questions of equality and freedom than either of the other two main political parties.

The Irish Labour Party was the least popular of the three major political parties in Ireland. It usually got between fifteen and twenty per cent of the votes in general elections, and was less united around its leaders than either of the other two. It had always been an opposition party and did not form part of the government until 1982, when it joined a coalition with one of the main parties.

In 1977, Mary ran as Labour Party candidate in a general election but lost, although narrowly. The same thing happened in 1981. In 1984 she failed to be appointed Attorney–General. Although she did not have to resign her seat in the Senate to be a candidate for the Dail [or legislature], elections for the Senate were always held shortly after the general elections for the Dail. But she never failed to win in any of those.

Mary resigned from the Labour Party in 1985. The reason for her resignation was that the Anglo–Irish Agreement about Northern Ireland, arrived at by the governments of Ireland and the United Kingdom in the same year, had been made without any consultation with the Unionists in Northern Ireland.

The Agreement included setting up a local Northern Ireland parliament to include all the political parties in Northern Ireland, and would allow the Irish government to give advice. The Unionists rejected the Agreement, because they had not been consulted in the first place, and also because they didn't want the Irish government being given any influence in Northern Ireland.

In 1999 the United Kingdom parliament embarked on a process of "Devolution". This meant giving some authority to the parts of the United Kingdom other than England, namely Scotland, Wales and Northern Ireland. Scotland got a parliament with considerable local authority, Wales got an "Assembly" with some, though less, local authority, and Northern Ireland was offered its own local parliament along the lines of the 1985 Anglo–Irish Agreement.

The offer of a Northern Ireland parliament initially led to difficulties with the Unionist party. The Unionists want Northern Ireland to remain part of the United Kingdom, while the various nationalist parties support Northern Ireland becoming part of the Republic of Ireland. Both the government of Ireland and the government of the United Kingdom insist that no change be made without the consent of the majority of people in Northern Ireland. Up to now, however, the majority have always been Unionist. The Unionists feared the inclusion of the republican parties in the local government, and the nationalists had doubts about the possibility of working with the Unionists.

Nonetheless, the Northern Ireland assembly seemed to afford the best possibility of establishing a permanent end to the conflict between the armed para–military forces on both sides. An enormous amount of political pressure was brought to bear on both the Unionist and Nationalist parties by the governments of Great Britain, Ireland and the United States and their leaders.

The Prime Ministers of the United Kingdom and of Ireland and the President of the United States as well as by the American mediator, Senator George Mitchell, urged the various political parties in Northern Ireland to agree to take part in the Assembly and to form a government. Trust was slow to develop, but eventually all but one (a splinter Unionist party) entered the Assembly and a coalition government was formed. How long it will last remains to be seen, but at least the process of reconciliation has started, and the outlook is better now than at any time since the establishment of Northern Ireland in 1922.

The 1937 Constitution of Ireland contained an absolute ban on divorce. After the establishment of the Irish Free State in 1922, divorce was possible in theory but not in practice. A couple would have had to convince both of the houses of the Legislature to pass a private Bill allowing it.

In fact, when a number of such applications were made, even that remote opportunity was removed by law.

Under pressure from Bishops of the Catholic Church, the prohibition of divorce was strengthened by being included in the 1937 revision of the constitution. This meant that divorce could only be made legal if first the legislature passed a Bill allowing it, and then the majority of the population voted for it.

Mary opposed this majority viewpoint. The constitutional ban on divorce, in her opinion, was due to the intrusion of the Catholic Church into politics. It resulted in limitations on freedom of conscience and behavior. Furthermore, since divorce was possible for persons living in Northern Ireland, it reinforced the fears of Protestants of living in a Church–dominated society in Ireland, and therefore made the eventual re–unification of the country less likely.

In 1986 Mary Robinson introduced a Bill to change the constitution on the matter of divorce. But in a national referendum, the proposal to allow divorce was defeated.

A Pro–Life Amendment Campaign (PLAC) began in 1981 in Ireland, with the object of having a ban on abortion inserted into the constitution. Abortion was already illegal under a 1861 law, still in effect then, but again, its inclusion in the constitution would make it extremely difficult to legalise it.

Before the 1981 general election, the Pro–Life group had managed to get each of the three political parties to agree to start the process leading up to a referendum on the subject; the referendum was finally held in 1983, and passed by a majority of two to one.

Mary believed the inclusion of the ban on abortion

in the constitution increased the differences between the laws of the Irish Free State and those in the North of Ireland, and it emphasized the controlling role of the Catholic Church in matter of morals and the laws implementing them.

It was not as though Irish Catholic women were not able to have abortions; it meant only that they had to travel either to the North of Ireland or to England to have them.

Information about availability of abortion in the U.K. was hard to come by and was subject to censorship. Mary Robinson got nowhere with her political attempts to alter the legal attitude.

Similarly her efforts to have the law outlawing contraception (birth control) rescinded were fruitless. She introduced in the Senate a Bill permitting contraception. This was defeated three times in 1971, in 1972 and again in 1974. Government legislation on the same subject, more restrictive, was also defeated.

However it must be said that the laws against contraception and divorce were eventually changed, and had it not been for Mary's bravery in forcing debates of these unpopular and controversial subjects, the eventual solutions would have been delayed even longer.

In introducing her Bill in the Senate to legalise contraception, she went against her parents' wishes, who were seriously embarrassed by their local bishop preaching against the Bill in their local church in their presence, and who had to face the objections of their neighbors and friends. In addition, her parents as loyal Catholics were opposed to contraception.

She also faced the much more formidable opposition of the Catholic Church. It had never hesitated to intervene in political matters which impinged on morality, about which it considered itself the only (and infallible) authority.

It had opposed, and caused to be defeated, a proposal to establish a state "mother and child" health scheme, for fear that contraceptive advice might be given, or that doctors might, under the scheme, be involved with women patients in discussion about sex, and family life. However times were changing, and people were becoming less convinced that they should not think for themselves about these issues.

In 1979 the Dail passed a Department of Health Bill allowing for limited availability of contraceptives, and in 1985 virtually abolished the remaining restrictions on their use. People were convinced that Mary had played a critical part in bringing all this about, and arguments for and against her would be heard for many years to come.

## THE LAWYER EMERGES: CHAPTER SEVEN
### The Law and its Opportunities

In contrast to her difficulties in the field of politics, the legal arena was one in which Mary had significant success. This was in large measure due to her personality and her training.

She had learnt from the U.S. that decisions in court cases could result in laws being changed by Congress, and that the Federal courts could bring about changes in Federal and State laws. She would use the Irish courts and constitution as well as the European courts and the European Convention on Human Rights to change the laws in Ireland.

Mary's focus was on equality and human rights, which were to become her major professional passions through her career. She was more successful in getting new laws enacted or old laws changed through her activity as a lawyer than she had ever done through politics.

She did this by becoming involved in cases of abuse of justice and of human rights. Some of the time she risked unpopularity by taking a minority position, but justice, not popularity, was her aim. For purposes of illustration, here some of the kinds of cases that involved injustice.

In the 1980s, women working for the Telephone company were being paid less than men, even though their work was more valuable than that of the men. There was an anti–discrimination law in effect at the time which stipulated that men and women should be paid the same for work of equal value. When challenged by Mary Robinson in court on the question, the government lawyers tried to rely on the technicality that the law covered only work of equal value, but when Mary took it to the European Court, that Court in 1988 had no hesitation in calling the government position absurd.

The government–owned airline Aer Lingus had the policy of forcing women employees to resign if they got married. Presumably this was for the usual reasons that other companies discriminated against married women: they were likely to have children, and the company would have to give them maternity leave, and the women would give their children priority ahead of their work for the company. It took a long struggle by Mary to have the policy overturned by the courts, but finally the airline company was forced to change its policy in 1990

An interesting case involved her husband and herself when she first became a Senator. If a Senator died, his wife was entitled to a widow's pension from the Senate. However in the case of a female Senator such as Mary, if she died her husband would not get a corresponding widower's pension. This struck Mary as unequal treatment, so she went to court to insist that husbands of female Senators should have pension rights on the same basis as the pension rights of widows of male senators. This case was resolved in 1979 in her favor.

Another but different kind of equality case involved income taxes paid by married couples, which were higher than if the couples were single. Mary again took this on as an equality issue, and had to take it to the Supreme Court before the government lost the case.

A very similar equality issue was taken by Mary also as far as the Supreme Court, in which she claimed that married couples should have the same social welfare benefits as unmarried couples. She won this case also.

The Supreme Court seem to have little hesitation, in

the face of Mary's arguments, in holding against the government. In 1973, a married woman was prevented by government action from importing contraceptives. In her particular case, her health and possibly her life were in danger if she were to become pregnant. The Supreme Court agreed that the woman's constitutional rights were being infringed. The following year the government introduced legislation allowing contraception. Although the proposal was defeated in that year, it was passed in 1979.

Another case revolved around the right of a woman to get legal aid in a civil matter having to do with her asking for a full legal separation from her husband, the nearest thing in Irish law at the time to a divorce. Mary had to go to the European Court of Human Rights, which found in 1979 that the Irish government had violated the European Convention of Human Rights.

Mary was president of CHERISH, an organization defending the rights of single mothers, from 1973 to 1990, and provided legal advice to it over that period of time. CHERISH lobbied for single mothers' rights to children's allowances and housing, and this was finally granted by the coalition government in 1973.

Roy Johnston sued the State on the grounds that he and his common–law wife had an illegitimate daughter, and the constitution, in protecting the Family, gave him the right to a divorce in order to found a family. Mary lost this case in the European Court of Human Rights which found that the Irish Constitution did not include any right to a divorce. However it found that the daughter's rights were being infringed by certain legal disabilities applying to "illegitimate" children which did not apply to "legitimate" ones. This decision came in 1986. The Status of Children

Act, enacted in 1987, removed discrimination against illegitimate children.

In 1977 David Norris brought legal action against the State arguing that criminalization of homosexuality (making homosexual behavior punishable by imprisonment) under the Offenses against the Person Act was unconstitutional. In 1981 a similar case in Northern Ireland went to the European Court of Human Rights which held that homosexuals were protected under European law. Mary argued that the decision in the latter case should apply to the Norris case. The Irish Supreme Court in 1982 threw out Mary's argument, saying that the Convention of Human Rights was not part of Irish law. The European Court of Human Rights in 1988 agreed with Mary. In 1993, homosexuality was decriminalized by the Irish parliament.

The Well Woman Centre in Dublin was sued by a Right–to–Life group for providing information on abortion. The Irish courts upheld the Right–to–Life group, but the European Court of Human Rights held that it was a free speech issue which was guaranteed in the European Human Rights Convention, and awarded damages.

Another free speech issue surrounding the censorship as "indecent and obscene" of an Irish Family Planning Association booklet about contraception; Mary represented the Irish Family Planning Association against the Censorship Board in the Supreme Court and won.

She represented the father of an illegitimate child who wasn't consulted before his child was adopted. This case was lost in the Irish courts, but won much later at the European Court in Strasbourg.

In view of the fact that European Courts were such an important part of Mary's ammunition in getting human

rights abuses corrected in Ireland, it is quite understand-
able that she and her husband Nicholas went on to found
the Centre for European Law at Trinity College in 1988.

Much of the legal work which Mary did was routine and
did not attract headlines, but it was recognized that she
had made herself a champion of those who were suffering
under bad law or insensitive bureaucracies.

# HIGH HONORS ACHIEVED: CHAPTER EIGHT

Mary makes her Mark

The Presidency of Ireland, until Mary Robinson ran for that office, had been pretty well determined by the main political party, Fianna Fail, which had nominated all the candidates who became Presidents since the office was established in 1937.

The Presidency, from a practical point of view, had no importance at all. Although the President was in theory the head of state, the presidency did not have a tenth of the visibility or influence of the Queen of England, even in Ireland, and nothing remotely approaching the real power and importance of the President of the United States.

For seventeen years there had not even been an election, and with the exception of Douglas Hyde, the first President, every President had been previously a Fianna Fail prime minister or politician. But in 1990, the Labour Party decided to put forward a candidate.

In the beginning, they did not expect to win. The aim was simply to increase the party's share of the popular vote. They took for granted that the Fianna Fail candidate, Brian Lenihan, would win. He was personally extremely popular, a decent man, and likely to make a good President.

The Labour Party was torn by personal and political quarrels, and the first candidate nominated was not Mary, but Noel Browne, the proponent of the "mother and child" scheme which he had introduced in the Parliament. However he was not the choice of the Labour Party leader, Dick Spring, who preferred Mary.

The issue was forced to a vote in the Party, which Mary won hands down. It was not a good beginning, and as the Presidential campaign got under way, support from the Labour Party and from Dick Spring was not always enthusiastic. However he had asked Mary to become the Labour Party candidate.

But in spite of Mary's preference for the Labour Party, she was not willing to run as the candidate for any political party, feeling rightly that as the President was supposed to be above politics, she would do better to run as an independent. In spite of Dick Spring's disappointment over this, he did round up the necessary twenty members to nominate her.

When he first asked her to run for office, she was reluctant, since she had resigned from the Senate the previous year; she and Nick had established the Centre for European Law a year before that, and her legal career in Europe was fulfilling its early promise. However Nick was in a way more ambitious for her than she was, and persuaded her to go for it.

Mary had learnt from her lack of success in running for political office, and this time she was determined to win. Nick was a tremendous help to her campaign, not merely because of his personal support, but also because of his wisdom in recognizing bad advice given to her by her advisers, of whom there were many, maybe too many.

Mary started her campaign early, even before the other two parties had decided on their candidates. She traveled all over the country, visiting little villages and towns, some of which had never seen any candidate for any political office before. She was already well known, and needed to get rid of the feminist and radical image that some people had of her. She had the same problem twenty years earlier when she had been a candidate for the Senate.

This time she had a lot of public relations people advising her.  Some of the advice was helpful, some was not.  She made mistakes, but her opponents made more and worse ones.  Since so many of her supporters had volunteered their services for free, the cost of her election campaign had cost one tenth of that of her principal opponent.

Her husband appeared with her on television and came over very well.  She softened her image, appeared less like a lawyer but more feminine, and her genuine interest in people and their problems came across in her public appearances.

Mary knew she had to get women to vote for her.  In her favor were her efforts over the years in fighting for equality for women, and this paid off.  Still, in the first round the Fianna Fail nominee, Brian Lenihan, gained more votes than either Mary or the candidate of the second–largest party, who came in third.  However his second–preference votes brought Mary into the lead, so she was elected President in November 1990.

The reaction in Ireland to her election was extraordinary; she had been very popular among women voters, less so among men, and of course her election was applauded by the members of all the organizations founded to help the poor and distressed.

Her inauguration took place in December 1990.  The inauguration ceremony was attended by a lot of women, representatives of women's organizations, trade unionists, organizations to help the homeless, disabled, students, young people, environmentalists etc., all of whom Mary had helped and supported in various ways.

There were also Northern Ireland political leaders from

all parties, including Unionists. In her inauguration speech Mary dedicated herself to people of Irish descent all over the world (the "Fifth Province"), people in the North of Ireland, and those living on the margins of society.

## MARY'S CHALLENGE—TRANSFORMING THE PRESIDENCY: CHAPTER NINE

An Office for All of the People

Mary Robinson moved into Arus an Uachtarain, the official residence of the President, in December 1990. This house had been, since 1782, the residence of the Governor–General (the representative of the British Crown in Ireland) until 1937, when it became the official residence of the President.

Virtually nothing had been spent on the upkeep of the house over the years. It was a mess, and was extremely dilapidated. The staff were elderly , and the atmosphere uncongenial, to say the least.

Mary got them replaced, mostly by younger and more active people. This resulted in terrible publicity make worse for political reasons. Mary was represented as hypocritical about her concern for the elderly and the unemployed, even though she made sure that the staff obtained other jobs. She wanted to make the house into a place where everybody would feel welcome, particularly people whom no one had even thought of inviting before. For example, the "Travellers".

The Travellers used to be known as Tinkers. They were not Gypsies (Romanies), but native Irish made homeless over the previous centuries by evictions, and lived on the margins of society. They lived in groups of extended families, traveling the roads in caravans, carts and make–shift carriages with tents. They earned their living by begging and selling tin pots and plates which they made themselves. Now largely settled in communities, they were not liked or trusted by their neighbors, who were inclined to suspect them of theft and other petty criminality. They were a bit like the "Untouchables" in India, totally isolated from the rest of the community.

Mary had come to their rescue as early as 1980, when she had forced a local authority, through court action, to provide public housing for a woman traveller whom it had evicted. Mary invited Traveller women to her official residence many times, and refused to allow public attention to be diverted from their problems.

It was inevitable that women's organizations would figure prominently among her guests, both from the Republic and from Northern Ireland. Ulster Unionists and nationalists were invited and came, because it was clear that Mary had meant what she said: she intended to be President of all sections of the Irish community.

She was seen as someone who understood and could sympathize with the Northern Unionists because the English tradition in Ireland was not alien to her, and members of her own family had been to a certain extent involved in English affairs. She and her husband had always believed that the Irish heritage involved more than the Gaelic heritage alone, and that the English and Anglo–Irish influences in Irish history and current life should be treasured also. She arranged to have a museum set up inside Arus an Uachtarain which included the period since 1782 when the Viceroys of Ireland, and later the Governor–Generals had lived in the house before her.

Mary continued to show highly visible support of community and voluntary groups, prisoners, the homeless, Aids organizations, the unemployed, children's charities and organizations helping the disabled. She took practical measures to promote equality of women included insisting on women military and women police at the Arus.

She continued to provide general support for the equality of women. She also conducted the office of President with due formality and reserve where and when it was appropriate to do so.

The Labour Party felt that Mary had been ungrateful to them, since she meant what she said about being independent. The Government party, Fianna Fail, under the leadership of Charles Haughey, was upset because she was the only President who had not had Fianna Fail's blessing. And she had beaten their candidate. They saw her as a challenge to the role that Haughey, the Prime Minister, had previously assumed. He de–emphasized the role of the previous President Patrick Hillery by not financially supporting the President, who had for a long time had to pay for the meals of the staff out of his own pocket.

Charles Haughey was a dominant figure, with a dismissive attitude towards the presidency. The constitution says that : "No power or function conferred on the president by law shall be exercisable or performable by him save only on the advice of the Government." Haughey interpreted this to mean that the President could do practically nothing without the approval of the government.

Mary believed that the constitution referred only to the President's right to refuse to dissolve the Dail, to refer a Bill to the Supreme Court to test its constitutionality and to address Parliament or the nation on matters of national importance. In other areas, such as speeches and media interviews, she believed she was free to follow and use her own judgment, although she couldn't leave the country without the permission of the government.

Mary attended events for the Rape Crisis Centre and

for Third World development agencies to raise funds. She chose her own secretary, replacing her predecessor's secretary, and she appointed Bride Rosney as a major adviser. Haughey objected to Mary's St. Patrick's Day message being broadcast across the U.S. by the Irish Tourist Board as part of a promotional package.

Mary gave nearly a hundred interviews in her first year as president to Irish and foreign newspapers. When the Dalai Lama came to Ireland in 1991, she wanted to invite him to Arus an Uachtarain, but in the face of official opposition, arranged to meet him at a special exhibition of Oriental Art. The Government told her that this would be "very unhelpful". However she met the Dalai Lama in spite of that, and Haughey backed off.

Although as President she could not leave the Republic without the consent of the government, she had no intention of being confined to Ireland, and a list of her foreign travel makes interesting reading. In 1991 she made her first visit as president to England, to open the European Bank for Reconstruction and Development. In 1992 she went to Belfast in Northern Ireland.

In the same year she made a State visit to France, went to Somalia and immediately after to the United Nations headquarters in New York to talk about the famine and the refugee problems in Somalia. In 1993 she went to England to attend a memorial service for two boys who had been killed by I.R.A. bombs, and the following month to Buckingham Palace to meet the Queen.

She returned to Belfast where she met Gerry Adams, leader of Sinn Fein, which was the nationalist organization seen as speaking for the I.R.A. In 1994 she went on official visits to the United States, Canada, South Africa, Zambia,

Zimbabwe, Tanzania and Rwanda.

In 1995 there were State visits to South America, including Argentina, Chile and Brazil, there was another visit to Rwanda, a State visit to Japan, and she received the Prince of Wales in Dublin.

In 1996, she made State visits to Britain, South Africa, and the United States. In 1997, her last year as President, she returned to Rwanda, to Northern Ireland, and made her first visit to the Vatican where she met the Pope.

The Irish people in general were pleased with the recognition Mary got for herself as well as for Ireland. Most of the countries had never seen an Irish president before, and still fewer a woman president. It was perhaps inevitable that she would feel a little more relaxed outside Ireland, and a little more unguarded in her comments.

Since she was under such scrutiny her comments were blown out of all proportion, and came in for some criticism at home. After seeing the Queen in Buckingham Palace, she went to Belfast where she was criticized for meeting and shaking hands with Gerry Adams, the leader of Sinn Fein. Under the circumstances of their meeting, it would have been impolite not to have done so.

Similarly when in South America, she was criticized for not drawing attention to the miserable conditions of the poor in some of those countries, but as the guest of their governments, it would surely have been out of place to have done so.

In Japan, she made a comment concerning the "Framework Document" about Northern Ireland written by both of the British and Irish governments. She commented to the effect that she understood how the Unionists might feel that their identity was being undermined by it. The press in Ireland made an issue of this, taking it as a criticism of the Irish government and an intrusion into politics, which it was not intended to be.

But over–all, however, Mary's foreign trips were a real success.  She represented Ireland, not as it once had been nor as it never was, but as it had become.  The Irish people were proud of her, and since she represented them well, of themselves as well.

What did Mary Robinson achieve as President?  She enhanced the position of women in Irish society, both by being President and by her support of the rights of women in practical ways.  It is worth noting that her successor as President is also a woman.

Mary made the office of President much more significant in Irish politics, no longer just a figure–head.  She drew attention to the problems of minorities and of the disadvantaged of the Republic and in Northern Ireland.  Through her visits to Third World countries and to the United Nations, she promoted awareness of the human misery which prevails in poverty–stricken parts of the world, and the need for rich western countries to help through the United Nations agencies.

She maintained the agenda she had pursued throughout her career, focusing on human rights above all, in Ireland and in the entire world.  Just as her Senate experience and her legal career had prepared her for the Presidency, so her achievements as President of Ireland prepared her for the next stage in her life, as the United Nations High Commissioner for Human Rights.

# FROM IRELAND TO THE WORLD: CHAPTER TEN
Important work at the United Nations

Mary Robinson's emphasis on Human Rights throughout her life can be attributed to many things, but perhaps most of all to the fact that she is a thoroughly decent person and the idea of living contentedly while millions of others are living in misery and poverty is foreign to her.

What are Human Rights? Essentially they are what people need, and have a right to have, in order to live decent lives. The American Declaration of Independence speaks of the right to life, liberty and the pursuit of happiness. But they have been more extensively described by others in the "Universal Declaration of Human Rights" formulated by the United Nations in December 1948 and adopted in principle by virtually every government in the world since then.

They were enumerated by Mary Robinson in her report to the Economic and Social Council of the United Nations in Geneva on 27th July 1999. Very briefly, they consist of freedom from fear and want, decent living conditions, the right to work, the right to education and to health services and social security. Other rights spelled out are the right to a fair trial if accused of any crime, and the right to have a representative government and to be able to participate in political activity if a person wishes to do so.

The number of people in the world who do not enjoy basic rights is staggering; hundreds of millions are starving. Nearly a billion people, for lack of even elementary education, are illiterate, and are unable to read or even sign their names. Billions lack basic sanitation; more than a billion do not have clean water to drink, and more than a billion do not have adequate housing.

In many countries, millions of people have an income of less than one US dollar a day. What basic human rights can they enjoy on these wages?

Nowhere are these rights more important than in the case of children, who are most vulnerable to the loss of these rights, and most damaged if they are denied, as they are in many countries. Poverty and war, including civil war, does terrible things to children.

Millions of children in the past ten years have been killed, many more than that seriously injured, even disabled. Children have been forced to take part in military operations, and apart from these horrors, children are exploited as workers and servants and are forced to engage in prostitution.

While most of these abuses occur in the underdeveloped Third World countries, some of them are not unknown in the "developed" countries of Europe and North America, including the United States.

Poverty denies children basic rights in developed countries and also denies them decent housing and living conditions, and opportunities for education.

Poverty does not usually lead countries to attack other countries, but certainly is a factor in rebellions against governments which do not represent the majority of the people. It is these lessons which surely led Mary Robinson to become, as she has, a champion of human rights.

Mary believed that the advantages she enjoyed carried with them the obligation to use her intelligence and education for the benefit of society in general. And, in particular, for its least successful members.

Although coming from a small country town in the west of Ireland, a country which was uninvolved in the wider international issues of the time, she has made a significant difference both to her own country and to the world.

The impartial and universal protection of human rights became to her what religion is to the devout, a matter of constant reflection and action. In her country of Ireland, she was able to use the law to successfully change long–standing traditions which supported injustices and discrimination. She succeeded in turning the Irish Senate and the Presidency of Ireland, purely ceremonial institutions, into ones which made a difference to the life of her time and to future generations.

Her appointment as United Nations Commissioner for Human Rights in 1997 is particularly appropriate, as a result. She has always seen human rights as universal and indivisible and inseparable from human life.

## CAREER HIGHLIGHTS: CHAPTER 11
Mary's Achievements

The importance and the impact of Mary Robinson's career is surprising given her failure, despite repeated attempts, to get herself elected or appointed in Ireland to any offices other than those designed to be without effective power. The offices she held were capable of attracting attention to the views of the office–holders on important subjects, but in themselves were not vehicles through which major changes could be implemented.

Indeed a catalog of her political initiatives lists failure after failure: failure to get elected, failure to get laws adopted or the constitution changed. But many of the measures she championed, however, were later put into effect by others; they would claim the credit, but she had been the originator.

Mary was far more successful as a lawyer than as a politician. Again her successes were in combating injustice and discrimination. She fought for couples of mixed religion to adopt children, equal treatment of men and woman as jurors and as surviving spouses of members of the Senate. It is noteworthy that prior to her efforts, women were favored in both these areas; her focus was on equality, not preference.

Access to information about abortion was another issue she took up. After initial defeats in the Irish courts, by going through the European Commission and the European Court of Human Rights, she managed to get the Irish courts' decisions overturned as infringing guarantees of free speech and freedom of information.

It was her election as President of Ireland, the first woman President, that catapulted her into the international sphere. Not merely had no woman ever run for that office, no woman had ever even been considered as a possible candidate. None of the main Irish political parties supported her campaign; they had their own candidates to promote. She did not have the financial backing that the political parties' candidates had, and she spent on her campaign one–tenth of what her main opponent did.

Very few political experts thought she had even a remote chance of winning, and yet she won, against all predictions. It is perhaps a measure of the impact she had as President that her successor in that office was also a woman.

Mary won the Presidency because she had the intelligence to realize and to come to terms with her own disadvantages in the race. She was the outsider, so she started her campaign long before either of the two other candidates. She had less money, therefore she could spend less on advertising, so she traveled around the country more, spoke to more people in person.

In Irish politics, it had always been a man's world, so she appealed to her natural allies, women, without whose support she could never have been elected. Up to that time, politics in Ireland had always been fiercely partisan, based on the experiences of the civil war. She was able to appeal to those who could get beyond recent and not so recent history, religious differences and concentrate on the purely human aspects of current problems.

Her election as President changed people's attitudes in Ireland about politics. Up to that point, the Presidency had been a gift of the political party in power, with one exception given to a former Prime Minister belonging to that party. Mary Robinson ran for election and the office of the Presidency as an independent, without the support of any political party, against their candidates. She won, proving for one thing that people could and did think differently from the politicians they had elected, and that people wanted their President to be something more than a rubber stamp. They had elected as President someone who had a mind of her own, who didn't think like any of the political parties expected her to think, and who didn't act like any previous President had acted.

As President she was extremely popular, except with the professional politicians. She continued to play her part in bringing light and reasonableness into the somewhat murky dialogue of Irish politics, and helping people move away from the traditional Irish and Irish—American view of their history as victims of oppression.

All that is not to say that the Irish had not been oppressed over the centuries by English laws, some of which bore startling resemblances to Nazi laws concerning the Jews in Germany in the 1930s after Adolf Hitler's take—over of power. The Irish language had been virtually outlawed, and began its inevitable decline to a dead language, no longer spoken or even understood by the vast majority of the Irish in Ireland and overseas.

To her credit, Mary Robinson made efforts to learn it, although she never became as proficient in it as she became in French, in which she was fluent. But she had reached the point of realizing, as the Israelis did, that a preoccupation with past injustices was counter—productive. Ireland had become a modern European nation, and had to work with other European nations, including England, just as Israel had learned to work with Germany, and that there was no point in going back, holding on to attitudes which were no longer helpful or relevant to the current situation.

She reached out to both Nationalists and Unionists in the North of Ireland, visited the Queen, entertained the Prince of Wales in Dublin, and in a sense anticipated the current peace process in Northern Ireland, which is being strongly supported by both the Irish and British governments now. She was always ahead of her time, always somewhat impatiently waiting for the rest of the world to catch up. It would not have been surprising if she had manifested an attitude of moral and intellectual superiority to the common run of people, especially those in political circles, but she was always a surprising person, and showed no trace of such an attitude in public life.

In 1997, at the end of her tenure as President of Ireland, she had been considered a candidate for the office of Secretary–General of the United Nations, but this was not to be, probably to her relief. However her appointment as U.N. Commissioner for Human Rights gave her more opportunity than she would have had as Secretary–General to concentrate on doing what was of most interest to her, and she has been able to utilize her position as Human Rights Commissioner to promote justice and equality on a far wider scale than she had ever been able to do before.

Of course this is by no means the end of her story. At the end of this millennium she is still in her early fifties, energetic and forward–looking, with her abilities and convictions unimpaired, her influence growing. She is far too young to retire from the international scene, and has much too much to contribute to simply go away and write her memoirs. What she will do remains to be seen, but given her past record it will probably be something surprising, even amazing. All of us live in hope.

## APPENDIX: A BRIEF HISTORY OF IRELAND

While almost everything about Ireland is a matter of dispute, the generally accepted view about the origins of the Irish people is as follows: A few thousand years ago, the Celts, who occupied central Europe in a broad band stretching from what is now Russia to the shores of France and Belgium, Northern Spain and Portugal and had settlements in Northern Italy and in Asia Minor (modern Turkey), continued their expansion westward across the English Channel, taking possession of the British Isles.

It is probable that they spread to Ireland from Britain, although might also have come directly from the continent. The generally held opinion is that the first Celts arrived in Ireland between 500 B.C. and 400 B.C.

They found there a stone-age people whom they displaced, driving them to the remote areas of the west, southwest and northwest of Ireland. They called these people the "Tuatha De Danaan" (the people of the goddess Dana) and believed they had magical powers, and later believed they had become the fairies, leprechauns and banshees of folklore. Some of these people, however, undoubtedly intermarried with the invading Celts and are one of the many nations which contributed to the development of the Irish people.

The Celts in Ireland, the Irish, lived in communities of varying sizes, mostly related to each other, something like the clan system of Scotland, though not identical to it. They had legendary heroes equivalent to the Welsh King Arthur and his Knights of the Round Table, their Irish counterparts being Finn McCool and the Fianna, and in the North of the country, The Red Hand of Ulster. Legends from the pre-Christian period include the story of Queen

Maeve of Connaught and the cattle raid of Cualgne, the love story of Deirdre and Grannia, and the story of Tristan and Iseult, Iseult being an Irish princess. While they lived from agriculture, hunting was both a source of food and the principal masculine recreation.

There was also a good deal of fighting between the various little kingdoms. Like the Greeks in Homeric times, they had poets to recite histories and legends, they had judges to uphold laws, and druids who were a combination of priests and doctors. Of their religion we know practically nothing at all, except the names of some of their gods and goddesses, one of whom, Eire, gave her name to the country as a whole.

The Roman Empire never extended to Ireland, although Britain was part of it, and Christianity did not reach Ireland until the Roman Empire was on its last legs. Saint Patrick had been captured in Britain and enslaved by Irish raiders in Ireland. He escaped however, became a priest and subsequently a bishop, and returned to Ireland, probably around 450 A.D. with the intention of converting the Irish to Christianity.

While much of what is told about him is probably fiction, there was a real Patrick who founded the Christian church in Ireland, and it is remarkable that the Irish embraced Christianity so readily and held onto it so tenaciously. During the so-called Dark Ages after the fall of the Roman Empire, Irish clerics established monasteries in Ireland, Scotland, Britain and the continent, including Switzerland and Italy, and helped keep literacy alive during the "barbarian" invasions of western Europe.

While Ireland was spared the Anglo-Saxon occupation of Britain, it was subject to regular raiding by the Vikings over a period of about three hundred years ending in the eleventh century. The decisive event in ending the harassment by the Vikings was the 1014 A.D. battle of Clontarf. The Vikings also established settlements and towns on the coasts, the precursors of the present Dublin, Wexford, Waterford, Cork, Galway and some others, and over the course of time through intermarriage became an inseparable and indistinguishable part of the Irish people.

The Vikings also took over Normandy, and as Normans started to occupy Britain after the battle of Hastings in 1066 A.D. During the almost perpetual in-fighting between the little Irish kingdoms, one of the warring Irish kings, Dermot McMurrough, in 1172 A.D. called for help to one of the British Norman barons who was happy to oblige, taking a tract of land for himself as his price, and also marrying McMurrough's daughter.

He was followed by other Normans, and in short order Normans were occupying sizeable areas of Ireland. However following their pattern in Brittany and Britain, they were assimilated with or by the earlier inhabitants, and settled down as their equals, learning and speaking the Irish language, adopting Irish customs and laws, and generally becoming, as Queen Elizabeth I later complained, more Irish than the Irish themselves.

Although Ireland had been, in theory at least, a possession of the English crown since the twelfth century, in fact the English controlled only a small part of the country around Dublin (called The Pale) until the religious wars of the 16th and 17th centuries which effectively ended any Gaelic influence in the running of the country. The massacre by Oliver Cromwell's troops of the population of the town of Drogheda still lingers in the folk memory.

The Catholic Irish population was reduced to the status of tenants of the Anglo-Irish landowners who adhered to the established Protestant church.

Under the so-called Penal Laws of the 17th and 18th centuries, education of Catholics was forbidden either in Ireland or abroad; they could not own land, practice any profession, nor possess property of any value. They could not vote nor stand for any elected office, and were reduced to an impoverished, largely illiterate underclass. The disastrous famines of the mid-nineteenth century virtually halved the population through death from starvation and disease and from massive emigration to the United States, Canada, and Australia.

By the end of the 19th century there was little indication that the situation, although improved, would ever change, in spite of some futile opposition over the preceding few hundred years. Queen Victoria had made a triumphal visit to Ireland near the end of her reign, and Irishmen volunteered to join the British Armed Forces in large numbers during the 1914–1918 war against Germany. However resistance, though scattered and intermittent, had not entirely disappeared. In 1916 a brief armed rebellion in Dublin was followed by the trial and execution of its leaders.

This proved to be a terrible mistake. The majority of the Irish population, which had not been in the least sympathetic to the rebellion, was appalled by the executions. Acceptance of British rule in Ireland withered away, to be replaced by a carefully planned, ultimately successful rebellion which led in the year 1922 to the setting up of the Irish Free State, which was transformed in stages to the present Republic of Ireland. It is the Republic of Ireland that our subject, Mary Robinson, served as President from the years 1990 through 1997.

The Republic of Ireland does not include the whole country. By the treaty of 1922, six counties were excluded from the Irish Free State, to remain part of the United Kingdom, which they still are. The Unionist majority, descendants of the English and Scottish people settlers, unfortunately did not treat the Catholic minority fairly, and obvious discrimination in matters of housing, employment and justice was the order of the day.

Resistance increased, and at the end of the 1960s armed conflict broke out and the situation became increasingly confused. The I.R.A (Irish Republican Army), the U.D.F. (Ulster Defense Force, a Unionist para-military group), the R.U.C. (Royal Ulster Constabulary or police) and later the British Army all played a part in the violence that followed and which has continued until recent years. This period of violence is what became known in Ireland as "The Troubles".

While, at the time of writing, a cease-fire is in effect, all sides are well-armed and the situation is like a powder keg waiting to explode. Although the current British, Irish and American governments, as well as responsible politicians in Northern Ireland, are working in good faith to set up a viable representative government in the province, centuries of oppression and of mutual fear, hatred and distrust are not quickly overcome, and the future remains clouded.

## CHRONOLOGY

1944: Born, May 21st, in Ballina, County Mayo, Ireland.

1949—1954: Primary school in Ballina.

1954—1961: Secondary schooling at boarding school, Mt. Anville, Dublin.

1961—1962: "Finishing School" in Paris, France.

1963: Entered Trinity College, Dublin as law student, having won an entrance scholarship.

1967: Graduated from Trinity College with law degree and B.A.

1968—1969: attended Harvard University and gained LL.M degree there.

1969: Became Reid Professor of Constitutional and Criminal Law at Trinity College, Dublin. Elected to the Irish Senate as one of the Trinity College representatives.

1970: Marriage to Nicholas Robinson.

1971: Fails in first attempts to have Senate adopt a Bill allowing contraception.

1972: Challenges in court the constitutionality of ban on contraception.

1973: Irish Supreme Court supports Mary Robinson's contention that the ban on contraception is unconstitutional. Re–elected to Senate.

1974: Her second attempt to have Senate Bill on contraception adopted fails. Government legislation on the same subject is defeated in the Dail.

1975: Appointed lecturer in European Community Law at Trinity College, Dublin. Wins case in the Irish Supreme Court on men–women equality issue involving jury service.

1976: Government changes law on jury service in response to Supreme Court decision in 1975.

1977: Loses bid for Dail seat in general election, but is re–elected to Senate.

1978: Lose men–women equality case involving pension rights for spouses of members of the Senate.

1979: Wins the above 1978 pension case. Elected to Dublin City Council. Government passes legislation allowing for limited access to contraception

1980: Wins tax case involving equal treatment of taxation for married and unmarried couples.

1981: Loses another bid (her last) for election to the Dail. Re–elected to Senate.

1982: Re–elected to Senate in another general election.

1983: Resigns from Dublin City Council.

1984: Appointed a member of the International Centre for the Legal Protection of Human Rights, London. Efforts to have her appointed Attorney–General meet with failure.

1985: Anglo–Irish agreement on the future of Northern Ireland signed, subsequently criticized by Mary Robinson because the Northern Ireland Unionists were not consulted about it.

1986: Introduces Bill in the Senate to change Irish Constitution which since 1937 contained a clause forbidding divorce. Referendum confirms ban on divorce.

1987: Re–elected to Senate.

1988: Opens, with her husband, the European Law Centre at Trinity College, Dublin.

1989: Announces her decision not to run for election to the Senate again.

1990: Runs as independent candidate for election to the Presidency of Ireland with the support of the Labour Party. Wins the election and is inaugurated in the month of December 1990.

1991: State visit to Portugal. Council of State is appointed which includes, as the President's nominees representatives of disabled persons' organizations and women.

1992: Visits to France, Australia, Somalia and to the United Nations in New York.

1993: Visits to Scotland, and to London where she is received by Queen Elizabeth. Visits the United States where she meets President Clinton. Meets Gerry Adams, head of Sinn Fein, in Belfast. Prince Charles, heir to the throne of England, visits the President in Dublin.

1993: The post of High Commissioner for Human Rights is created by the United Nations.

1994: Visits to the United States, South Africa, Canada and Rwanda.

1995: Visits Japan and South America.

1996: State visit to the United States. Meets Queen Elizabeth in London on second visit to Buckingham Palace.

1997: Visits Rwanda, Great Britain. Received by Pope John Paul II at the Vatican. Announces intention of not seeking re—election as President of Ireland.

1997: Appointed United Nations High Commissioner for Human Rights.

## GLOSSARY OF TERMS

*Arus an Uachtarain:* The official residence of Irish Presidents since 1937. Previously, it had been the official residence of the (British) Governor–Generals of Ireland.

*Dail Eireann:* The government of Ireland (the Oireachtas) consists of the President, the Senate and the Dail. Members of the Dail are elected by the people using a system of proportional representation, which ensures that the political parties get a percentage of the Dail seats roughly proportional to their percentage of the popular vote in general elections. The Dail is the effective seat of political power and elects the Taoiseach (prime minister) and the other ministers of the government.

*European Court of Justice:* Properly known as the Court of Justice of the European Communities, established by the European Union. Decisions of the European Court of Justice can reverse decisions of the Irish Supreme Court.

*Fianna Fail:* A political party founded by Eamon de Valera in 1926. A political continuation of the faction which did not accept the treaty by which Ireland was divided in 1922 into the Irish Free State and Northern Ireland. It formed the government of Ireland from 1932 to 1948, and from 1957 to 1973, and currently. In 1990 its candidate for election to the Presidency of Ireland was defeated by Mary Robinson, who became President in that year.

*Indira Gandhi:* leader of the Indian Congress Party, and Prime Minister of India 1966–77; 1980–84.

*Ireland:* also Eire, the Republic of Ireland, the South of Ireland. Refers to the provinces of Leinster, Munster, Connaught and three counties of the province of Ulster, in all twenty–six counties which make up the independent republic.

*Northern Ireland:* six counties of the province of Ulster which form part of the United Kingdom of Great Britain and Northern Ireland, the capital of which is London and whose head of state is Her Majesty Queen Elizabeth II. At various times Northern Ireland has been ruled directly from London, at other times there has been a legislature elected by the people of Northern Ireland with limited powers of self–government. In December 1999 an assembly took office; this included members of the major political parties in Northern Ireland, including Unionists and members of Sinn Fein. It is to have some authority roughly equivalent to the Scottish Parliament set up in 1999.

*Queen Elizabeth 1:* Daughter of King Henry VIII, died 1603.

*Queen Cleopatra:* Queen of Egypt in the first century B.C. Egypt had been one of the provinces of the empire of Alexander the Great (of Macedon) and continued to be ruled by one of his "Epigoni" (successors) from whom Cleopatra was descended, until Egypt was incorporated into what was to become the Roman Empire, by Julius Caesar. Cleopatra's native language was Greek.

*Seanad Eireann:* The Irish Senate. Forty–three of its members are elected by local authorities, eleven nominated by the Taoiseach (prime minister), and six by the two universities. It can propose amendments to legislation, which can be accepted or rejected by the Dail, and can delay, but not prevent, the implementation of laws passed by the Dail. Mary Robinson was a member of the Senate as one of Trinity College's representatives from 1969 to 1989.

*Sinn Fein:* A political party which promotes the inclusion of Northern Ireland in the Republic of Ireland. Often it is seen as the political wing of the I.R.A. which is a para–military group declared illegal both by the United Kingdom and by the Republic of Ireland.

*Margaret Hilda Thatcher:* Prime Minister of the United Kingdom and currently a member of the British House of Lords with the title of Baroness Thatcher.

*Trinity College, Dublin:* The first university in Ireland, founded by Queen Elizabeth 1 as a Protestant university to support the establishment of British government and British law in Ireland.

*Unionist Party:* members of this party support the continuation of the inclusion of Northern Ireland in the United Kingdom.

*University College, Dublin:* Founded in the late 19th century and heavily influenced by the Roman Catholic Church until fairly recent times.

*World War II: 1939 to 1945.* The worldwide conflict which involved every major political power in the world. Mary Robinson, the subject of our book, was born in 1944.

## To Learn More

There are a number of publications that are useful in learning more about Mary Robinson. Her official biography is by Olivia O'Leary and Helen Burke.

O'Leary, Olivia and Burke, Helen. *Mary Robinson— The Authorized Biography.* London: Hodder Stoughton General, 1998.

While written for adults, it will provide further information about Mary Robinson as will another biography of her by John Horgan.

Horgan, John. *Mary Robinson: A Woman of Ireland and the World.* New York: Rinehart Press, 1998.

Several periodical articles have been written about Mary Robinson in her role as President of Ireland. An interesting article about her appeared in the April 15th, 1996 issue of The Nation.

Spillane, Margaret. *Should this Woman run the World?* The Nation, volume 262, page 11-16, April 15th, 1996.

An article by Mary Robinson in her new role as United Nations High Commissioner for Human Rights can be found in the UN Chronicle.

Robinson, Mary. *Saying what we mean. Meaning what we say. Together.* UN Chronicle, Volume 34, Number 4, page 24-27, 1997.

For more information about Ireland and its culture, you may find one of the following titles useful:

Browne, Terence. *Ireland: A social and cultural history 1922 to the present.* Ithaca: Cornell University Press, 1985.

Fraser, T. G. *Ireland in Conflict 1922–1998.* New York: Routledge, 1999.

O'Brien, Conor Cruise. *States of Ireland.* New York:

Pantheon Books, 1972.

On the internet, there are two web sites that are useful in providing information about Mary Robinson.

<www.irlgov.ie/aras>

<www.unhchr.ch>

The first is the web site of Arus an Uachtarain and provides biographical information about each of Ireland's Presidents and Mary Robinson. The second is the United Nations Human Rights web site, and provides information about the work and activities of this office.

# Index

Abortion, 8, 31

Adams, Gerry, 46, 47

Aer Lingus, 35

Anglo-Irish Agreement, 29

Anti-Semitism, 9

Architecture–Dublin, 26-27

Arus an Uachtarain, 19, 43, 67

Ballina, 6

Battle of the Boyne, 1690, 12

Belgium, 7

Boland, Eavan, 14

Bourke Family, 11

Bourke, H. C., 13

Browne, Noel, 39

Bruton, John, 19

Catholic Church, 8, 31-32

Centre for European Law, 38

Charles, Prince of Wales, 47

CHERISH, 36

Civil Rights Movement–United States, 17

Civil War, 7, 9

Cleopatra, Queen of Egypt, 5, 58

Clinton, Bill, 19-20

Cobh, 7

Contraceptives, 8, 23, 32-33, 36

Coyne, Anne, 14

Dail, 21, 33, 45, 67

Dalai Lama, XIV, 46

De Valera, Eamon, 6, 7, 17, 65

Declaration of Independence, 16, 49

Denmark, 7

Divorce, 8, 23, 30

Dublin, 26

Elizabeth I, Queen of England, 5, 68

Emigration, 16

Equal Pay for Equal Work, 34

Equal Protection Before the Law, 35

*European Bank for Reconstruction and Development, 46*

*European Convention on Human Rights, 34, 36*

*European Court of Human Rights, 34, 36, 37, 52*

*European Union, 19*

*Famines, 16*

*Fianna Fail, 7, 39, 45, 67*

*Gaelic, 9*

*Galway, 7*

*Gandhi, Indira, 5, 67*

*Germany, 7*

*Great Britain, 6, 29*

*Harvard University, 15, 17-18*

*Haughey, Charles, 45*

*Hillery, Patrick, 45-46*

*Holland, 7*

*Homosexuality, 37*

*Human Rights, 15, 28, 49-51*

*Hyde, Douglas, 9, 39*

*IRA see Irish Republican Army*

*Ireland–History, 6, 59-63, 67*

*Irish Constitution, 9, 30, 36*

*Irish Family Planning Association, 37*

*Irish Free State, 6, 10, 30*

*Irish Labour Party, 28, 39, 45*

*Irish Republican Army, 63*

*Irish Senate, 21-22, 68*

*Irish Student Law Review, 14*

*Irish Supreme Court, 19, 35, 45*

*Irish Times, 21*

*Irish Tourist Board, 46*

*Irish–United States, 17*

*Irish-Americans, 7*

*Johnson, Lyndon Baines, 18*

*Johnson, Roy, 36*

*Justice, Administration of, 19*

*Kennedy, John Fitzgerald, 17*

*Kennedy, Robert, 19*

*King, Martin Luther, Jr., 19*

*Leinster House, Dublin, 27*

*Lenihan, Brian, 39, 41*

*Marriage, 23*

*Mitchell, George, 30*

*Mount Anville (School), Dundrum, 12*

*Netherlands see Holland*

*Nobility–Great Britain, 10*

Normans, 11
Norris, David, 37
Northern Ireland, 8, 23, 29, 68
Northern Ireland–Peace and Mediation, 19, 29
O'Donnel Family, 11
Pojninska, Anita, 13
Presidents, 10, 39, 48
Presidential Powers, 45
Protestants, 8
Queenstown see Cobh
Religion, 8
Robinson Family, 25-26
Robinson, Mary–Achievements, 48, 52-55
Robinson, Mary–Children, 27
Robinson, Mary–Chronology, 64-66
Robinson, Mary–Foreign Travel, 46-48
Robinson, Mary–Presidential Campaign, 40-42
Robinson, Nicholas, 14, 21, 25, 40
Rosney, Bride, 27, 46
Royal Family–Great Britain see Nobility–Great Britain
Scotland, 29

Sexual Discrimination, 35
Sinn Fein, 46, 48
Spring, Dick, 39-40
Status of Children Act, 36
Switzerland, 10
Taxation, 35
Thatcher, Margaret Hilda, 5
Travellers, 43
Trinity College, Dublin, 9, 13-14, 21-22, 69
Unionist Party, 69
United Kingdom see Great Britain
United Nations, 46, 48-49
United States, 16
United States–Constitution, 17-18
Universal Declaration of Human Rights, 49
University College, Dublin, 14, 68
Vietnamese War, 1957-1975 18
Wales, 29
Well Woman Centre, Dublin, 37
Women–Civil Rights, 23
Women–Ireland, 41, 45, 48
Wood Quay, 27
World War II, 6